Secrets, secrets

Nola Turkington

Illustrated by Robin McBride

'Will you help me with my homework, Pini?' Rose asked her brother.

'I'm busy,' said Pini. He was hammering a nail into a piece of wood.

'What are you making?' asked Rose.

'A box,' her brother answered.

'Why?' asked Rose.

Pini sighed. His sister was always asking questions. She always had to know everything.

'Because it's a present, and I want to finish making it today,' he said.

'Who is it for?' Rose asked.

'Just someone,' replied her brother.

'Why won't you tell me?' demanded Rose.

Just then Mother called from the kitchen window.

'Rose, it's time to do your homework.'

Rose went inside.

Pini wiped his hands on his shorts. 'Great – she's gone now,' he thought. 'If I tell her the box is for Zolika, she'll keep asking me questions. Mother made me promise I wouldn't tell Rose about Zolika.'

Rose forgot about the wooden box. But the next morning, she saw Pini at the gate. He was talking to Msi, his best friend.

Pini gave Msi the wooden box he had made. He had worked hard on it, and it was now smooth and shiny.

'Why is he giving the box to Msi?' wondered Rose.

Rose thought about the box all day. She was cross with Pini for not telling her about it. Then she had an idea. 'Perhaps it's a present for Zolika.'

Zolika was Msi's older sister. She went to school in a big city. She had often looked after Rose when they were growing up.

When Rose arrived home, she said to her mother, 'Mother, is Zolika back home on holiday yet?'

For a few seconds Mother didn't answer. Then she said, 'Yes, Zolika is home.'

'Why hasn't she been to see us?' asked Rose.

'Zolika isn't well. She's in bed.'

'What's wrong with her?'

'I can't tell you.'

'Can I visit her?'

'No, she's too sick.'

'I could sit next to her bed and read her a story.'

'No,' said Mother firmly. 'You are not to go next door.'

Rose was upset. 'If she's sick, I must help her,' she said to herself.

After supper, Rose and her brother were watching TV.

Rose said, 'Mother says I can't visit Zolika. I'm not allowed to go next door. Can you visit Msi?'

'No,' Pini answered.

'Why?' Rose asked.

Pini shook his head. 'I can't answer that,' he said.

Rose was very cross. 'Secrets, secrets! No one ever tells me anything.'

The next day Rose cheered up because Enoch came home. Enoch was her oldest brother, and he ran his own transport business in the city.

That evening, the children told Enoch their news.

‘Did you know Zolika is sick?’ Rose asked him.

‘No,’ he said. ‘What’s wrong with her?’

Rose started to say she didn’t know, but Mother interrupted. ‘I’ll tell you later,’ she said. She looked worried. Rose knew that something was wrong.

The next morning, Mother called Rose. 'We have something to tell you,' she said.

Enoch said, 'Mother and I have talked about Zolika. Zolika has Aids. She is very sick. Mother was worried that you and Pini would catch the Aids virus if you visited her. But visiting a person with Aids is not dangerous. In fact, it is very important to care for friends who are ill.'

Mother added, 'I want to help our neighbours, but I am worried about our family. There is a lot I don't know about Aids because people just don't talk about it. I will ask Zolika's mother what we should do.'

That afternoon, Mother said to her neighbour, 'Can I talk to you about Zolika?'

Zolika's mother smiled. 'Come in,' she said. 'We must talk about Zolika. We're not ashamed of her illness – we want to do what is best for her. And it is not good to keep secrets about Aids. Everybody gets the wrong ideas and they're scared. That does not help anybody.'

'I was scared my children would catch the Aids virus,' Rose's mother admitted.

'In fact,' said Zolika's mother, 'you can't get the Aids virus just from being with someone who has it, or touching them, or sharing food, dishes, clothes or toilets. You will only get the virus if their body fluids mix with yours.'

'Body fluids?' said Rose's mother.

'I mean blood, semen or mother's milk.'

Zolika's mother went on, 'Most people get HIV from having sex without a condom. HIV turns into Aids. That's what happened to Zolika.'

She picked up some leaflets from the table. 'Look,' she said. 'We got these leaflets from the clinic. They tell you all about it.'

Rose's mother read all about HIV/Aids. She read that you can't get it just by being near someone or touching them. So when Rose came home from school the next day, her mother said, 'Would you like to visit Zolika?'

'Yes, please!' said Rose. She picked up one of her mother's magazines and went next door.

Zolika looked very thin and weak, but she sat up and hugged Rose. 'Thank you for coming,' she said. She told Rose all about her school, her boyfriend and her sickness.

When she got tired, Rose said, 'I've brought you a magazine. Can I read you a story?'

When she had finished, Rose noticed the box at the foot of Zolika's bed.

'This is the box Pini made,' she said. 'What are you going to put in it?'

'I call it my memory box,' said Zolika. 'I wanted something to put my special things in. You know I'm sick, and I can't go out. Now I can open the box and remember good times, and the people I love.'

She showed Rose what was inside. There was a photo of Zolika as a baby, an old drawing of her house, a tattered rag doll, and an old school report.

When it was time for dinner, Rose went back home.

'How was Zolika?' asked Mother.

'She is very sick,' said Rose, 'but I read her a story, and she liked it. She wants me to see her every day.'

'Can I visit Msi?' Pini asked.

'Yes,' said Mother. 'We must all do everything we can to help our neighbours.'

Rose smiled. 'I'm so glad there are no secrets any more!'

Let's talk

1. Why did Rose's mother want to stop her from seeing Zolika?
2. Why are many people afraid of talking about Aids?
3. Zolika's mother says it is not good to keep secrets about Aids. Do you agree with her? Why?
4. 'Knowledge is the best prevention against Aids.' What does this mean?